Teacher's Resource Book

American Headway 2

Matt Castle

John and Liz Soars

OXFORD

UNIVERSITY PRESS

OXFORD
UNIVERSITY PRESS

198 Madison Avenue
New York, NY 10016 USA

Great Clarendon Street
Oxford OX2 6DP England

Oxford New York

Athens Auckland Bangkok Bogota Buenos Aires Cape Town
Chennai Dar es Salaam Delhi Florence Hong Kong Istanbul
Karachi Kolkata Kuala Lumpur Madrid Melbourne Mexico City
Mumbai Nairobi Paris São Paulo Shanghai Singapore Taipei
Tokyo Toronto Warsaw

and associated companies in Berlin Ibadan

Oxford is a trademark of Oxford University Press

ISBN 0-19-437934-5

American Headway 2 Teacher's Resourse Book:
Editorial Manager: Shelagh Speers
Managing Editor: Jeff Krum
Editors: Pat O'Neill, Eliza Jensen
Art Director: Lynn Luchetti
Designer: Jennifer Manzelli
Art Buyer/Picture Researcher: Elizabeth Blomster
Production Manager: Shanta Persaud
Production Assistant: Zainaltu Jawat Ali

Printing (last digit): 10 9 8 7 6 5 4 3 2 1

Printed in China.

Acknowledgments

Cover concept: Rowie Christopher
Cover design: Rowie Christopher and Silver Editions

Illustrations by: Adrian Barclay, Phil Burrows, Kate Charlesworth,
Neil Gower, Tim Kahane, Karen Minot, Jeff Shelly, Harry Venning

*The publisher would like to thank the following for their kind
permission to reproduce photographs:* S. Bruty/Stone; P.
Enticknap/The Travel Library; K. Fisher/Stone; P. Francis/Stone;
G. Grigoriou/Stone; D. Hoffman/Rex Features; Hulton-Deutsch
Collection/Corbis UK Ltd.; K. Lahnstein/Stone; Popperfoto;
Retna Pictures Limited; Rex Features

Introduction

This Teacher's Resource Book contains 29 photocopiable activities and further ideas for you to use with *American Headway 2*. It has been written with two aims in mind:

- to give teachers additional material that reviews and extends the work in the Student Book

- to give students lots of extra speaking practice!

Students at the pre-intermediate level need lots of vocabulary and grammar input. Controlled skills work is also important to develop their reading, writing, listening, and speaking. But at the same time, it is also essential that they are given opportunities to "get active" and actually use their English in meaningful and relevant contexts.

The activities in this book are designed to help your students do this. They encourage students to talk about themselves, compare opinions and views about the world, and practice the kind of situations they are likely to encounter in real life.

In addition, every activity involves an element of teamwork. Students will need to work together to share or check information, and agree on outcomes or solutions. In other words, every activity encourages purposeful interaction where students need to speak and listen to each other.

Through role plays, language games, questionnaires, crosswords, and information-gap activities, students are also given the chance to build their confidence and introduce a more personal dimension to their learning.

How to use the photocopiable activities

Each activity starts with the following information:

Aim	the main focus of the activity
Language	the grammar/function practiced
Skills	Speaking, Reading, Writing, and/or Listening
Lesson link	suggestion for when to use the worksheet
Materials	notes for preparation of the worksheet

Pre-activity

These activities act as a warm-up before the students carry out the main activity. They act to remind students of the necessary language needed and to set the context.

Procedure

This section has step-by-step instructions for carrying out the main activity. Each main activity takes between 20 and 30 minutes and is suitable for most class sizes. (There are additional notes for larger classes.) For each activity there is a photocopiable worksheet. Some of the worksheets need to be cut up before handing them out to students.

Extension

After each main activity, there is a suggestion for an extension activity. These are generally writing activities that build on the language or topics covered in the main activity. These can be assigned for homework.

Contents

Worksheet	Description	Language
1.1 Asking questions for a minute	Board game to practice asking questions	Present Simple questions and answers
1.2 Perfect neighbors	Describing people and expressing opinions	Present Simple; Personality adjectives
2.1 Americans Abroad	Discussing cultural differences	Present Simple; Comparing and contrasting
2.2 Living with others	Completing and discussing a questionnaire on lifestyles	Present Simple questions and answers; Fluency practice
3.1 Prime suspects	Exchanging information on suspects' whereabouts to solve a crime	Past Simple and Continuous questions and answers
3.2 Fortunately . . .	Telling a story using cartoon strips	Past tenses
4.1 Shopping cart	Exchanging information to write a shopping list	Food vocabulary; *much/many*; *There is/are*
4.2 Are you a shopaholic?	Completing and discussing a shopping questionnaire	Present Simple
5.1 Future plans and ambitions	Exchanging information to complete fact sheets	Present Continuous for future plans; *would* for hopes/ambitions
5.2 *have*, *go*, and *come*	Playing dominoes to collocate nouns and verbs	Collocation of verbs *have*, *go*, and *come* with nouns
6.1 Superlative classmates	Completing a questionnaire about classmates	Superlatives
6.2 Vacation Getaways	Role-playing travel agents and vacationers	Comparatives; *What's . . . like?*; Fluency practice
6.3 The New York City bike race	Planning a route for a bicycle race	Prepositions of place and movement; Directions
7.1 The People's Biography	Role-playing an interview for a people's biography	Tense review; Asking and answering questions
7.2 Twentieth-century music	Reading about different musical eras and discussing significant facts	Past tenses
8.1 Baker's dozen	Completing a job crossword	*have to*; Job vocabulary
8.2 Chain card compound	Playing dominoes to make compound nouns	Compound nouns

Worksheet	Description	Language
9.1 Hot verb 4-squares	Playing a board game to revise verb phrases using *take, get, do*, and *make*	Verb phrases with *take, get, do*, and *make*
9.2 Hotel Headway	Board game to role-play hotel situations	Asking for information and making requests, booking a hotel room, etc.
10.1 The last time you felt . . .	A free-speaking activity based on feelings	Adjectives; Present and past tenses; Fluency practice
10.2 Eye witness!	Checking and comparing information in four eye-witness accounts	Asking for and giving information; Past tenses
11.1 The robbery	Telling a story from pictures	Passives
11.2 When and Where?	An interesting facts quiz	Passive questions: present and past
12.1 Problem doctors	Role-play giving advice	Second Conditional; Fluency practice
12.2 Hypothetical mingle	Discussing hypothetical situations	Second Conditional; Fluency practice
13.1 First day at college	Role-playing a first day at college	Fluency practice
13.2 The recruitment game	Discussing the best candidate for a job	Fluency practice; Tense review
14.1 Family feuds	Discussing seating arrangements for a feuding family	Fluency practice
14.2 The good-bye game	Role-playing saying good-bye in a variety of formal and informal situations	Fluency practice

1.1

Asking questions for a minute

Aim

To ask and answer questions about family, likes, hobbies, etc.

Language

Asking and answering questions
Present Simple

Skills

Speaking

Lesson link

Use after *Talking about you* SB p. 4

Materials

One copy of the worksheet for each group of four students

Pre-activity (10 minutes)

- Write these subjects on the board: *Town, Mother, Hobbies, Good friend, Father, English, Favorite food, School or work, Grandparents, Country, Vacations, Brothers or sisters, Good movies, Favorite music, Animals or pets.*

- Ask three or four students some simple questions, e.g., *What town do you come from? What's your best friend's name?*, etc.

- Divide students into pairs. Tell pairs that they can ask you questions about one topic each. Allow students a few minutes to think of as many questions as they can about their chosen topic. Answer all their questions.

Procedure (20 minutes)

- Explain that students are going to play a board game. When they land on a square they have to ask other members of their group questions related to that subject. The aim of the game is to ask as many questions as possible in a minute. (Make sure each group has a watch with a second hand to time the speaking student.) Tell the students that they should answer the "playing" student's questions as quickly as they can in order not to hold up the game.

- Divide students into groups of four and give each group a copy of the worksheet. Ask each student to choose a "marker," e.g., a coin, paper clip, etc., to move around the board.

- Students take turns tossing a coin to move around the board (heads = move one square, tails = move two squares). Students get a point for each question asked. The student with the most points at the end is the winner.

- Go around the room listening while the students are playing, and help as necessary. Do not correct students while they are playing but make a note of common errors and go over them with the whole class at the end.

Extension (5 minutes)

- Ask individual students to tell the class what they found out about one member of their group. They shouldn't say the student's name and the class should try to guess who is being described.

Asking questions for a minute

1.2

Perfect neighbors

Aim
To describe people and express opinions

Language
Personality adjectives
Present Simple

Skills
Speaking

Lesson link
Use after *Neighbors* SB p. 8

Materials
One copy of the worksheet for each pair of students

Pre-activity (5 minutes)

- Ask students what kind of building they live in, e.g., house, apartment, etc. Ask them about their neighbors, e.g., *Do you get along well with your neighbors? What annoys you about your neighbors?*

Procedure (15 minutes)

- Explain that students are going to look at 12 potential neighbors and decide whether they would be good neighbors. The criteria for their decisions should be based upon whether they would like quiet/friendly neighbors, neighbors with/without children, etc., and not on appearance or race.

- Divide students into pairs and give each pair a copy of the worksheet. (If you have an uneven number of students, make one group of three students.) Ask students to look at the 12 possible neighbors and discuss whether they could live next door to these people and explain why/why not, e.g., *I couldn't live next door to the woman in number 10 because she plays the violin. I'd like to live next door to the man in number 8 because he looks friendly. I wouldn't like to live next door to the family in number 2 because their children look noisy.* Go around listening and helping with vocabulary as necessary.

- Review students' responses as a class. Find out how many students could/couldn't live next door to each neighbor. Encourage students to explain why/why not.

Extension (10 minutes)

- Ask students to write down five things they would look for in perfect neighbors, e.g., *They are young. They aren't noisy. They invite me to lots of parties. They are friendly. They don't play loud musical instruments*, etc. Tell students to refer back to the 12 pictures for ideas about what they would/wouldn't like. Go around the room helping with vocabulary as necessary.

- Review students' responses as a class. What is the most/least popular quality for a perfect neighbor?

Could you live next door to these people?

Americans Abroad

Aim
To compare aspects of American culture with the students' cultures

Language
Comparing and contrasting
Present Simple

Skills
Reading and Writing

Lesson link
Use after *Living in the USA* SB pp. 14–15

Materials
One copy of the worksheet for each pair of students

Pre-activity (5 minutes)

- Explain that students are going to talk about cultural differences between the United States and their own country. Encourage students to tell you any differences they already know.

Procedure (25 minutes)

- Explain that students are going to complete a fact sheet for a company which caters to Americans who are moving abroad. Students provide the company with cultural information which will help the Americans in their new country.

- Divide students into pairs and give each pair a copy of the worksheet. Read through the introductory paragraph with the class and make sure students understand the activity.

- Ask students to read through the notes about U.S. culture. Explain any unfamiliar vocabulary. Does any of the cultural information surprise the students?

- In pairs, students think about how their culture differs for each category and complete the fact sheet. (If the class is mixed nationality, pairs of students can interview each other and complete the fact sheet with their partner's answers.) Go around the room helping with vocabulary as necessary.

- Review answers as a class. Lead this into a discussion about personal experiences abroad.

Extension (10 minutes)

- Students imagine they are tourists from the United States visiting their country. They write a postcard home describing any cultural differences they have found interesting.

Americans Abroad is a new company to help American people live in different countries. Here are some examples of U.S. culture. Please make notes about your country under the different headings.

Restaurants
Americans usually pay a 15% tip. But they expect good service.

Your country _____

_____

_____

Food
You can buy food from any country in the world.

Your country _____

_____

_____

Language
Many Americans expect to do everything in English.

Your country _____

_____

_____

Work
Americans work long hours. Many start very early in the morning and don't finish until late in the evening.

Your country _____

_____

_____

Health
Hospitals in the U.S. are private and Americans have private medical insurance to pay for their health care.

Your country _____

_____

_____

Holidays
Most Americans only have two weeks' vacation a year.

Your country _____

_____

_____

Education
American children have to go to school from 6 to 16, and they need to study for 12 years to get a high-school diploma.

Your country _____

_____

_____

Cities
Many stores in the U.S. stay open 24 hours a day, 7 days a week. You can get anything you want, any time you want.

Your country _____

_____

_____

Travel
A cheap way to travel long distances in the U.S. is by bus.

Your country _____

_____

_____

Crime
The crime rate in many U.S. cities is quite high.

Your country _____

_____

_____

2.2

<table>
<tr><td>

Aim

To discuss living preferences, habits, and hopes for a roommate situation and to negotiate compromises

Language

Asking and answering questions

Negotiating

Tense review

Fluency practice

Skills

Reading and Speaking

Lesson link

Use after *You drive me crazy* SB p. 16

Materials

One copy of the worksheet for each student

</td></tr>
</table>

Pre-activity (5 minutes)

- Ask students about their living situations: *Do you live with your parents? / with other family members? / with friends? / by yourself?*

- In small groups, ask students to think of two advantages and two disadvantages of living with other people.

- Review ideas as a class.

Procedure (20 minutes)

- Explain that students are going to share an apartment with the other students in their group. First, they are going to complete a questionnaire. Then, in groups, they are going to discuss their living preferences with their new roommates. Together they have to draw up a plan of action that will help them live together in perfect harmony!

- Give each student a copy of the worksheet. Read through it quickly with the class and explain any unfamiliar vocabulary.

- Individually, students complete the questionnaire.

- Divide students into groups of three or four. Students compare their answers, e.g., *I don't like doing the dishes, but I like cooking. It really annoys me when people play loud music late at night. I think we should share the food bill but not the telephone bill,* etc. Go around the room listening and helping as necessary. Encourage students to make compromises where their habits differ greatly.

- Review the results as a class. Ask students how happy they think they would be sharing an apartment with the other members of their group. Ask students what issues remained unresolved. Can the rest of the class offer solutions?

Extension (10 minutes)

- Ask students to write four rules for their new roommates, e.g., *Don't play loud music after ten o'clock. Wash your dishes every day,* etc.

- In small groups, students compare their rules and decide who they could share an apartment with. Review answers as a class.

LIVING WITH OTHERS

You

1. Are you a private person?   Yes ☐   No ☐

2. Do you like to talk a lot?   Yes ☐   No ☐

3. Do you like to stay at home a lot?   Yes ☐   No ☐

4. Do you have a quiet life?   Yes ☐   No ☐

5. Do you often invite friends home?   Yes ☐   No ☐

Tidying

How often do you . . .

1. clean the bathroom?   Every day ☐   Once a week ☐   Other _____

2. clean up?   Every day ☐   Once a week ☐   Other _____

3. do the dishes?   Every day ☐   Once a week ☐   Other _____

Cooking

1. Do you like eating with your friends?   Yes ☐   No ☐

2. Do you like taking turns cooking the evening meal? Yes ☐   No ☐

What time?

What time do you . . .

1. normally use the bathroom?   _____

2. eat meals?   breakfast _____   lunch _____   dinner _____

3. go to bed?   during the week _____   on weekends _____

4. get up?   during the week _____   on weekends _____

How often?

How often do you . . .

1. play loud music?   Every day ☐   Once a week ☐   Never ☐

2. watch TV?   Every day ☐   Once a week ☐   Never ☐

3. use the telephone? Every day ☐   Once a week ☐   Never ☐

Bills

Do you think everybody should pay the same amount of money for . . .

1. the telephone bill?   Yes ☐   No ☐

2. the electricity bill?   Yes ☐   No ☐

3. the food bill?   Yes ☐   No ☐

3.1 Prime suspects

Aim

A role-play activity where students work out when a murder was committed and the identity of the murderer

Language

Past tenses

Skills

Speaking

Lesson link

Use after *The Burglars' Friend* SB pp. 18–19

Materials

One copy of the worksheet cut up for each group of six students

Pre-activity (10 minutes)

- Ask individual students: *Where were you last night? What were you doing? Who was with you?*

- In pairs, students discuss where they were and what they were doing last night between 7:00 and 9:00. They say how they could prove this by saying who they were with and/or who saw them during this time. As a class, students compare what they did and how strong their alibis are.

Procedure (30 minutes)

- Explain that students are going to act out a roleplay in which somebody was murdered last night. Set the scene: Arthur Pink, owner of the 24/7 Bar was killed between 7:00 and 9:00 last night. Tell students that there are six suspects and their task is to find the murderer.

- Divide students into groups of six and give each student a different role-card: A–F. Tell students that they were all in the area when Arthur was killed, and one person in each group is the murderer! They have information about where they were, and more information in an "alibi chart" which explains where and when they saw other people that evening.

  Note: The murderer is Harry Lazio. Give this role to stronger students. Their aim is to conceal where they were when they killed Arthur (between 8:00 and 8:15). However, they must truthfully explain where other people were.

- Individually, students read their role-cards. Walk around the room and help with any new vocabulary.

- Then students talk to the other people in their group. They ask who each person saw that night (including when and where) in order to complete their "alibi chart." The innocent suspects have an alibi for every minute of the evening. However, the murderer doesn't have an alibi during the short time when he/she visited and killed Arthur. Go around the room listening and helping as necessary.

- Review answers as a class.

Extension (10 minutes)

- Students write a report explaining how the innocent suspects could explain where they were at the time of the murder, and the movements of the murderer during that fateful night! Go around the room helping with vocabulary as necessary.

A   Joey

On the night of the murder I was in Ron's Pool Hall between 7:00 and 7:30. Then I went to the 24/7 Bar to meet my girlfriend, Edna. We had a couple of drinks, then left at 8:00. We had something to eat in Pizza Piazza, and then I went home at about 9:00.

▼ These are the people I saw that evening:

	7:00	7:15	7:30	7:45	8:00	8:15	8:30	8:45	9:00
Joey	Ron's Pool Hall	→	The 24/7 Bar	→	Pizza Piazza				→
Lolita	Ron's Pool Hall		The 24/7 Bar						
Edna			The 24/7 Bar	→	Pizza Piazza				→
Peter Sharp	Ron's Pool Hall	→			Pizza Piazza				
Molly May									
Harry Lazio	Ron's Pool Hall	→							

✂ -

B   Edna

On the night of the murder I was in the 24/7 Bar. I arrived at 7:00 to meet my boyfriend, Joey. He was half an hour late so I sat by myself until he finally arrived at 7:30. We had a few drinks then went to the Pizza Piazza at 8:00. We were there for an hour, and then I went home.

▼ These are the people I saw that evening:

	7:00	7:15	7:30	7:45	8:00	8:15	8:30	8:45	9:00
Edna	The 24/7 Bar	→			Pizza Piazza	→			→
Joey			The 24/7 Bar	→	Pizza Piazza	→			→
Molly May	The 24/7 Bar	→							
Lolita		The 24/7 Bar	→						
Harry Lazio									
Peter Sharp					Pizza Piazza				

C Lolita

On the night of the murder I was working in Ron's Pool Hall until 7:15. Then I went to meet Edna in the 24/7 Bar. I only stayed for half an hour, and then I went back to the Pool Hall to meet some friends. We stayed there until 8:30, and then we caught the bus downtown where all the best clubs are.

▼ These are the people I saw that evening:

	7:00	7:15	7:30	7:45	8:00	8:15	8:30	8:45	9:00
Lolita	Ron's Pool Hall	The 24/7 Bar	→	Ron's Pool Hall		→	Bus into town	→	→
Peter Sharp	Ron's Pool Hall			Ron's Pool Hall		Ron's Pool Hall			
Molly May		The 24/7 Bar			Ron's Pool Hall	→	Bus downtown	→	→
Harry Lazio	Ron's Pool Hall					Ron's Pool Hall			
Edna		The 24/7 Bar	→	→					
Joey	Ron's Pool Hall		The 27/7 Bar						

✂ --

D Peter Sharp

On the night of the murder I was playing pool in Ron's Pool Hall until 8:00. Then I went to Pizza Piazza because the owner, Antonio Lazio, owed me money. I told him to give me $1,000, but he only had $200! I went back to Ron's Pool Hall again at 8:15 and I stayed there for the rest of the night.

▼ These are the people I saw that evening:

	7:00	7:15	7:30	7:45	8:00	8:15	8:30	8:45	9:00
Peter Sharp	Ron's Pool Hall	→		→	Pizza Piazza	Ron's Pool Hall	→		→
Molly May						Ron's Pool Hall			
Harry Lazio	Ron's Pool Hall	→		→		Ron's Pool Hall	→		→
Edna					Pizza Piazza				
Joey	Ron's Pool Hall	→	→		Pizza Piazza				
Lolita	Ron's Pool Hall			Ron's Pool Hall		Ron's Pool Hall			

E Molly May

On the night of the murder I was in the 24/7 Bar from 7:00 until 7:30. Then I went to Pizza Piazza for a sandwich. I was there for half an hour, and then I walked over to Ron's Pool Hall for a cup of coffee. I stayed until 8:30, and then I took the bus into town where I live.

▼ These are the people I saw that evening:

	7:00	7:15	7:30	7:45	8:00	8:15	8:30	8:45	9:00
Molly May	The 24/7 Bar	→	Pizza Piazza	→	Ron's Pool Hall	→	Bus into town	→	
Harry Lazio				Pizza Piazza		Ron's Pool Hall			
Joey									
Lolita		The 24/7 Bar			Ron's Pool Hall	→	Bus downtown		→
Peter Sharp						Ron's Pool Hall			
Edna	The 24/7 Bar	→							

✂ --

F Harry Lazio

You are the murderer! At the beginning of the evening you were drinking in Ron's Pool Hall. At 7:45 you went to see your brother Antonio at Pizza Piazza. He gave you a gun. Then you walked into the 24/7 Bar at 8:00. Arthur was alone and you shot him before he had a chance to escape. Then you went back to Ron's Pool Hall for the rest of the evening. Don't tell anyone that you are the murderer! Here are the other people you saw that evening. Make sure nobody finds out that you were in the 24/7 Bar at 8:00!

▼ These are the people I saw that evening.

	7:00	7:15	7:30	7:45	8:00	8:15	8:30	8:45	9:00
Harry Lazio	Ron's Pool Hall	→		Pizza Piazza	The 24/7 Bar!!!	Ron's Pool Hall	→		
Edna									
Molly May				Pizza Piazza		Ron's Pool Hall			
Lolita	Ron's Pool Hall					Ron's Pool Hall			
Joey	Ron's Pool Hall	→							
Peter Sharp	Ron's Pool Hall		→			Ron's Pool Hall			→

Photocopiable

3.2

Aim

To review *fortunately* and *unfortunately* using cartoon strips

Language

Past tenses

Skills

Speaking and Listening

Lesson link

Use after *fortunately/unfortunately* SB p. 21

Materials

Two copies of each story for each pair of students (one of each story cut up with the prompts removed)

Pre-activity (10 minutes)

- Write *fortunately* on the board. Ask: *How many syllables does it have? (four) Where is the /tʃ/ sound? (fortunately) How many /ə/ sounds are there? (two: fortunately) What's the opposite of fortunately? (unfortunately).*

- Tell a class chain story similar to those in the Student Book. Say: *I lost my bag last week.* Invite a student to add a sentence to your story starting with *Fortunately*, e.g., *Fortunately my purse wasn't in the bag.* Then invite another student to add another sentence with *Unfortunately*, e.g., *Unfortunately my house keys were in the bag*, and so on.

Procedure (25 minutes)

- Explain that students are each going to put a story in order and then, using prompts, tell the story to their partner.

- Divide students into pairs. Give a cut-out (and out of order) version of *Malcolm and Sarah's Vacation* to Students A and *The Terrible Bank Robbers* to Students B (both without the prompts).

- Give students several minutes to put their story in order. Go around the room monitoring progress.

- Give students the prompts (out of order) which accompany their story. Students match the prompts with the pictures.

- Now give Students A a complete version (including the prompts) of *The Terrible Bank Robbers* and Students B a complete version of *Malcolm and Sarah's Vacation.*

- Organize your class so that each Student A is paired up with a Student B. Students now take turns telling their story using *fortunately* and *unfortunately*. The listening student (who is looking at the complete version of the story) follows the story to see if their partner's predicted sequence is correct. Go around the room listening and correcting as necessary.

Extension (10 minutes)

- Ask your students to think of an event in their lives that was good but then became bad, or was bad but then became good.

- When everybody is ready, divide the class into groups of three or four. In their groups, each student explains as much as he/she can remember about the events.

alarm / not go off

arrive / airport in time

flight / delayed

two seats left / earlier flight

sit / next to the Adams family

The Adams family / different resort

bus / flat tire

tour guide / taxi to the hotel

hotel / awful

room available / hotel next door

The Adams family / same hotel

Big Norman   Bugsy   Arthur   Ron

The Terrible Bank Robbers / get lost

Bugsy / plan of the bank

plan / out of date

Shopping cart

<table>
<tr><td colspan="2">

Aim

An information-gap activity where students decide what food they need to buy

Language

Food Vocabulary

How much/many . . . is there?

There's a lot/ a little.

There are a lot/ a few.

Skills

Speaking

Lesson link

Use after *The weekend shopping trip* SB pp. 26–27

Materials

One copy of the worksheet cut in half for each pair of students

</td></tr>
</table>

Pre-activity (5 minutes)

- Write the food items below on the board. In pairs, students talk about the prices for these items in their own country. (Explain that *dozen* means *twelve*.) Review answers as a class.

eggs	*89¢ per half dozen*
ketchup	*$1.00 a bottle*
butter	*$2.50 for 500g*
olive oil	*$2.99 a liter*
bananas	*25¢ each*
toilet paper	*$1.99 for 6 rolls*
toothpaste	*$2.39 a tube*
bread	*$1.59 a loaf*
coffee	*$1.99 a jar*
apples	*35¢ each*
milk	*$1.29 a liter*
sugar	*85¢ a kilogram*

- Tell students the average prices in the United States for each item. Write the prices on the board next to the food items. Leave the items and prices on the board as students will need to refer to them in the Extension activity.

Procedure (20 minutes)

- Explain that students are going to work out what they need to buy. Their partner can see what they have in their home and will tell them if they need to buy certain items.

- Divide students into pairs. Give Students A worksheet A, and Students B worksheet B.

- In pairs, students take turns asking and answering questions to see which items on their list they need to buy, and which can wait, e.g., *How many eggs do I have? Two. How much butter do I have? A lot/A little,* etc. Go around the room listening and making sure students use *much/many* correctly.

- Review answers as a class.

Extension (10 minutes)

- When everybody has finished, divide students into groups of four and tell them that there is a problem. They have run out of all the items on their list. They have only $10 to spend. In their groups, students decide which items to buy.

- Review as a class to see what each group has chosen.

Teacher's notes

A

Student B's home

SHOPPING LIST:
Eggs
Ketchup
Butter
Olive Oil
Bananas
Toilet Paper

B

Student A's home

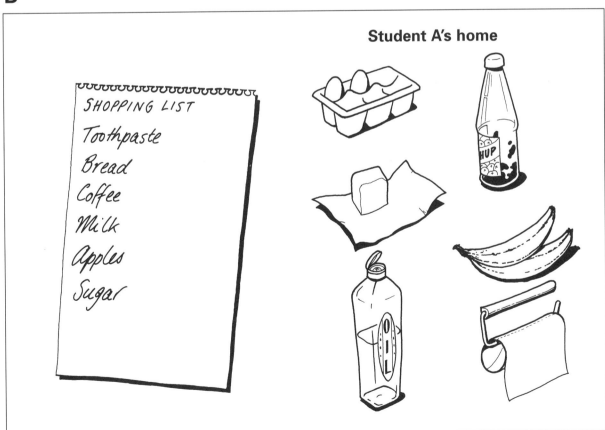

SHOPPING LIST
Toothpaste
Bread
Coffee
Milk
Apples
Sugar

4.2

Are you a shopaholic?

Aim
To complete a questionnaire to determine attitudes about shopping

Language
Present Simple

Skills
Reading and Speaking

Lesson link
Use after *The best shopping street in the world* SB p. 30

Materials
One copy of the worksheet for each student with the results removed and cut up

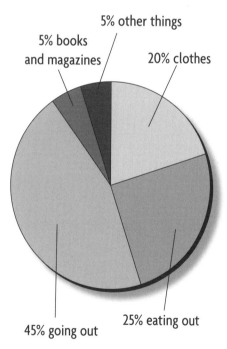

5% other things

5% books
and magazines

20% clothes

45% going out

25% eating out

Pre-activity (10 minutes)

- Write these statements on the board:
    put it all in the bank
    spend it all on . . .
    put $ . . . in the bank, and spend the rest on . . .

- Tell students they have each won $1,000. In small groups, students discuss what to do with their money. Review students' ideas as a class.

Procedure (20 minutes)

- Write *alcoholic* on the board. Ask students what it means. Then write *shopaholic* on the board. Can students figure out what it means? Explain that students are going to complete a questionnaire to find out if they are shopaholics.

- Give each student a copy of the worksheet. Give them several minutes to read through it and to check any items of vocabulary.

- Individually, students complete the questionnaire.

- Divide students into groups of four. Give a different results card to each member of the group. Students read their card to the group.

- Review the results as a class. Do students agree with the "answers"?

Extension (10 minutes)

- Ask students to work out what percentage of their money they spend on clothes, eating out, going out, buying books and magazines, and other things. They should calculate the proportions and make a pie chart (see left) with their calculations. It is not necessary to discuss amounts of money each student has to spend here as we are dealing only with percentages of a total sum in this activity.

- In small groups, students compare their pie charts.

Are you a shopaholic?

What kind of shopper are you? Check (✔) the response which best describes how you feel.

1 If I want something, I usually buy it.
   A Agree ☐   B Disagree ☐

2 New clothes make me feel more attractive and confident.
   A Agree ☐   B Disagree ☐

3 Possessions tell me a lot about a person.
   A Agree ☐   B Disagree ☐

4 Credit cards are a bad idea.
   A Disagree ☐   B Agree ☐

5 I like hunting for bargains.
   A Agree ☐   B Disagree ☐

6 I like to think carefully before I buy something.
   A Disagree ☐   B Agree ☐

7 When I buy a present for someone, I buy what I would like for myself.
   A Agree ☐   B Disagree ☐

8 Everything I buy, I use or wear a lot.
   A Disagree ☐   B Agree ☐

9 My home is full of things I don't really need.
   A Agree ☐   B Disagree ☐

10 I still like things I bought years ago.
   A Disagree ☐   B Agree ☐

---

7 or more As

You are a shopaholic! You like to spend money and often buy things you don't need. Shopping is a hobby for you.

5–6 As

Shopping helps you to feel good about yourself. You think that lots of possessions can make you more desirable to other people.

3–4 As

You go shopping only when you need to buy a specific thing. You don't lose control or buy lots of expensive things.

2 As or fewer

Possessions aren't important to you. Be careful! Other people might think you are too strict. It might be a good idea to relax more when you go shopping.

5.1

Aim

To exchange information to complete plans and ambitions fact sheets for four people

Language

Present Continuous for plans
would for hopes/ambitions

Skills

Speaking

Lesson link

Use after *Hopes and ambitions* SB pp. 34–35

Materials

One copy of the worksheet cut in half for each pair of students

---

Pre-activity (5 minutes)

- Write *tonight, next week, next summer,* and *in ten years' time* on the board. Tell students your plans and hopes/ambitions, e.g., *Tonight, I'm going to the movies. Next week, I'm going to the dentist. Next summer, I'd like to go to India. In ten years' time, I'd like to live near the ocean.*

- Ask individual students to tell you about their plans for tonight and next week, and their hopes and ambitions for next summer and in ten years' time, e.g., *What are you doing tonight? What would you like to do next summer?* etc.

Procedure (20 minutes)

- Explain the activity to the class. Students are going to ask and answer questions to complete the fact sheets about the plans and hopes/ambitions of four people.

- Divide students into pairs. Give Students A worksheet A, and Students B worksheet B.

- In pairs, students take turns asking and answering questions to complete the fact sheets. Go around the room listening and making sure students use the correct tense for the questions, e.g.:

  Q *What's Paula doing tonight?*
  A *She's doing her homework.*
  Q *What's Paula doing next week?*
  A *She's going to Tokyo on vacation.*
  Q *What would Paula like to do next summer?*
  A *She'd like to graduate from college.*
  Q *What would Paula like to do in ten years' time?*
  A *She'd like to travel around the world.*

- Review answers as a class and check that everyone has filled in the fact sheets correctly.

Extension (10 minutes)

- Ask students to make two blank plans and ambitions fact sheets in their notebooks. Students complete the first fact sheet with information about themselves. Go around the room helping with vocabulary as necessary.

- Divide students into new pairs. Students take turns asking each other about their plans and ambitions and complete the second fact sheet. Go around the room listening, correcting, and helping as necessary.

A

Nick — Plans: Tonight: Go to the movies; Next week: Visit his friends. Hopes and Ambitions: Next summer: Go to India; In 10 years' time: Buy a house.

Paula — Plans: Tonight: Do her homework; Next week: Go to Tokyo on vacation. Hopes and Ambitions: Next summer: Graduate from college; In 10 years' time: Travel around the world.

Jesse — Plans: Tonight; Next week. Hopes and Ambitions: Next summer; In 10 years' time.

Thomas — Plans: Tonight; Next week. Hopes and Ambitions: Next summer; In 10 years' time.

B

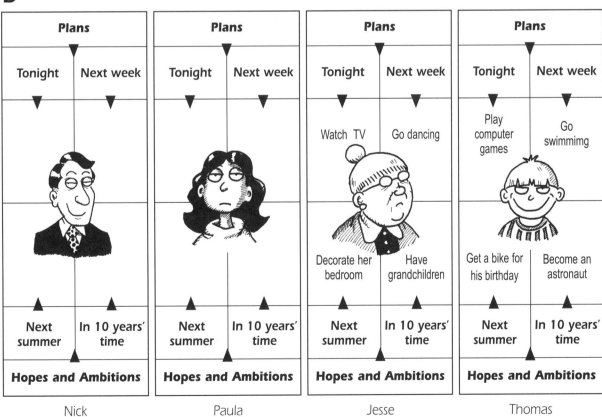

Nick — Plans: Tonight; Next week. Hopes and Ambitions: Next summer; In 10 years' time.

Paula — Plans: Tonight; Next week. Hopes and Ambitions: Next summer; In 10 years' time.

Jesse — Plans: Tonight: Watch TV; Next week: Go dancing. Hopes and Ambitions: Next summer: Decorate her bedroom; In 10 years' time: Have grandchildren.

Thomas — Plans: Tonight: Play computer games; Next week: Go swimmimg. Hopes and Ambitions: Next summer: Get a bike for his birthday; In 10 years' time: Become an astronaut.

5.2

have, go, and come

Aim

To play dominoes to collocate nouns with the verbs *have, go,* and *come*

Language

Collocation of verbs and nouns

Skills

Speaking

Lesson link

Use after *Hot verbs* SB p. 40

Materials

One copy of the worksheet cut up for each pair of students

Pre-activity (5 minutes)

- Write *have, come,* and *go* on the board. Brainstorm nouns which go with each verb, e.g., *have dinner, come home early, go to bed,* etc.

Procedure (15 minutes)

- Explain that students are going to play dominoes. On one half of the domino is a verb and on the other half is a preposition, a noun, or noun phrase. Students play by matching the verb with the correct preposition, noun, or noun phrase.

- Divide students into pairs and give each pair a mixed-up set of dominoes.

- Students place the dominoes face down on the table. Each student then takes seven dominoes and hides them from his/her partner's view.

- Pairs flip a coin to see who starts. This student places a domino on the table. The other student chooses one of his/her dominoes and places it next to the domino to make a correct match. This student then makes a sentence with the verb phrase, e.g., *Come on! We're late. The movie starts in ten minutes,* etc. The game continues. If a student cannot place a domino, he/she has to take a domino from the table and miss a turn. The winner is the student who gets rid of his/her dominoes first. Go around the room monitoring the games and correcting any mistakes.

Answers

Come back!   go out   come at eight o'clock   have a cold   Go away!
Come on! We're late!   have a good time   go swimming
come over for dinner   have time   go to a restaurant   Come here!
have lunch   go for a walk   have a meeting   go abroad
come in   have a headache

Extension (5 minutes)

- In small groups, students link a set of dominoes into a full circle. Introduce a competitive element by racing the groups against each other.

a headache	come	back!	go	out	come
at eight o'clock	have	a cold	go	away!	come
on! We're late!	have	a good time	go	swimming	come
over for dinner	have	time	go	to a restaurant	come
here!	have	lunch	go	for a walk	have
a meeting	go	abroad	come	in	have

Superlative classmates

<table>
<tr><td>

Aim

To complete a questionnaire based on fact and opinion

Language

Superlatives

Skills

Speaking

Lesson link

Use after *Comparatives and superlatives* SB pp. 43–44

Materials

One copy of the worksheet for each student

</td></tr>
</table>

Pre-activity (10 minutes)

- Do a general knowledge superlatives quiz with the class. Divide students into groups of four to six. Read out the following questions for students to answer. The group with the highest number of correct answers wins.
  1. *What is the longest river in the world? (Nile)*
  2. *What is the largest desert in the world? (Sahara)*
  3. *What is the largest ocean in the world? (Pacific)*
  4. *What is the largest island in the world? (Greenland)*
  5. *What is the smallest country in the world? (Vatican City State)*
  6. *What is the nearest planet to Earth? (Venus)*
  7. *What is the largest city in the world? (Mexico City)*
  8. *What is the busiest airport in the world? (Heathrow, London)*

Procedure (20 minutes)

- Explain that students are going to interview each other to complete a questionnaire. The questionnaire is divided into two sections: the first is a fact section where all students in the class should have the same answer; the second is a more personalized section based upon the individual student's opinion.

- Give each student a copy of the worksheet. Give them time to read through it and to check any items of vocabulary. Quickly ask students the questions they will use when they are interviewing each other, e.g., *How tall are you? How many countries have you visited?* etc.

- Students interview each other, writing the answers in their notebooks and then complete both sections of the questionnaires. (If your class is large, you can divide students into groups of about six students to ask the questions. Then each group passes on their results to the next group, and so on.)

- Review answers as a class. Encourage students to justify their answers when there are differences of opinion.

Extension (15 minutes)

- Students write a short report summarizing the results of the questionnaire.

SUPERLATIVE CLASSMATES

Fact

1. Who is the tallest?

Name: _____

Height? _____

2. Who is the youngest?

Name: _____

Age? _____

3. Who speaks the most languages?

Name: _____

How many? _____

4. Who has visited the most countries?

Name: _____

How many? _____

5. Who plays the loudest musical instrument?

Name: _____

Which? _____

Opinion

1. Who has the most exciting hobby?

Name: _____

What is it? _____

2. Who has visited the most interesting country?

Name: _____

Where? _____

3. Who has the most interesting reason for learning English?

Name: _____

Reason? _____

4. Who wears the most colorful clothes?

Name: _____

5. Who has the most unusual pet?

Name: _____

What is it? _____

6.2

Vacation Getaways

Pre-activity (10 minutes)

- Write *Virgin Gorda, British West Indies; Paris, France; Hong Kong,* and *Athens, Greece* on the board. Ask: *Have you visited any of these places? What do you know about each place?* Brainstorm information.

Procedure (40 minutes)

- Explain the activity to the class. One half of the class are travelers who are trying to decide where they want to go on vacation. These students will complete a questionnaire to help them decide where to go. The other half of the class are travel agents who are trying to sell them different vacation trips. The travelers will talk to four travel agents and ask questions about each place.

- Divide the class into two groups: travelers and travel agents. Give the vacation questionnaire to the travelers. Students complete the questionnaire individually. Then they think of questions they would like to ask the travel agents and write them at the bottom of the questionnaire.

- While the travelers are completing their questionnaires, hand out a destination summary (A, B, C, or D) to each travel agent. Travel agents read their summaries and prepare to talk about their city. Go around the room helping with vocabulary as necessary.

- Now it's time for buying and selling! Travel agents set up their stalls around the classroom and try to sell their vacation destination to the travelers who visit them. (You may want to let travelers work in pairs and travel agents work in small groups.) Tell the travelers to describe the kind of vacation they are looking for and to ask as many questions as they can about each city before they make their final choice, e.g., *What's the nightlife like? What excursions do you offer?* etc. Encourage them to record details of each vacation in their notebooks. Encourage the travel agents to be as persuasive as they can to sell their destination. Tell them that the excursions are very important to sell (they get a 10% commission). Go around the room listening and helping as necessary.

- Review results as a class. How many students decided to go to each destination? Encourage them to justify their choices.

Extension (15 minutes)

- Travelers write a postcard home describing their vacation. Travel agents write a destination summary for their hometown. Go around the room helping with vocabulary as necessary.

Vacation Getaways

We can help you to choose the right vacation! Complete this form before you speak to our travel agents. The information you give will help them to recommend the best destination for you.

What kind of vacationer are you?

Put a number in each box (3 = always, 2 = sometimes, 1 = never).

I like to keep busy and active.	☐	I'm happiest when I'm shopping.	☐
I like to relax and do very little.	☐	I like sitting in cafes watching the world go by.	☐
I prefer large, noisy cities.	☐	I want to see lots of historical monuments and buildings.	☐
I like small towns with a slow pace of life.	☐	At night I like to go to good restaurants.	☐
I want to stay in the city all the time.	☐		
I like to escape into the countryside.	☐	I stay up late and go to bars or nightclubs.	☐
		I go to bed early to prepare for the next day.	☐

Use this space to write some questions you would like to ask each travel agent, e.g., *Tell me about . . . , What's the nightlife like? What is there to do during the day? Are there any historical monuments? Are the restaurants and clubs good?* etc.

Buys of the MONTH!

Virgin Gorda, B.W.I.

Paris, France

Hong Kong

Athens, Greece

All half price!

A

Virgin Gorda, British West Indies

A relaxing place to sit back and enjoy the view!

Visitors to Virgin Gorda, a tiny island in the British West Indies, will learn how much fun it can be to do nothing at all. The weather is always perfect, the people are friendly, and there's no noisy nightlife to spoil the peaceful mood. Relax on an uncrowded beach all day and enjoy the best seafood in the world all evening!

RECOMMENDED

- Small, picturesque seaside towns
- Beautiful beaches
- Slow pace of life

Hotel Fact File: Large rooms (most with ocean view). Excellent small restaurants at most hotels.

Excursions: Sunset Sail $45
Enjoy the rich colors of the sunset at their best
Whale watching $45
See these ocean giants in their natural setting
The Baths $20
A day trip to the most beatiful spot on the island

B

Paris, France

Enjoy the excitement of this world capital!

Many people think that the only time to visit Paris is in the spring. But whenever you go, you'll find plenty to see and do. This giant city is a true world capital, full of famous museums, world-class restaurants, elegant stores, and interesting neighborhoods. You'll want to spend every moment of your vacation soaking in the sights and sounds of this fascinating city.

RECOMMENDED

- Famous art museums
- Ancient historical sites
- Relaxing sidewalk cafes

Hotel Fact File: Comfortable rooms (all with TV and air conditioning), very good locations in central Paris.

Excursions: City Tour $40
The best way to see museums and art galleries
Versailles Tour $40
Visit the magnificent palace of Loius XIV
Paris by Night $40
See famous cafes and nightclubs after dark

C

Hong Kong

Enjoy great shopping and fine dining in this bustling city!

Visitors to Hong Kong will find everything they need for an exciting vacation in this city that never sleeps. Within Hong Kong there is fabulous food, great shopping malls, busy open-air markets, and fascinating street life. Everything is here within a few minutes' walk or a short taxi or bus ride from your hotel.

RECOMMENDED

- Duty-free shopping
- Street market bargains
- 9,900 different restaurants

Hotel Fact File: Comfortable rooms
(many with mountain or harbor views).
Excellent restaurants near most hotels.

Excursions: Land and Sea Tour $75
Includes lunch at a floating restaurant
Hong Kong at Night $90
Enjoy dinner, dancing, and more
Fabulous Food $100
Eat at three superb restaurants in one night

D

Athens, Greece

The oldest capital in Europe where history becomes reality!

When you go to Athens, you are visiting the birthplace of Western civilization. You can see the places where Plato and Socrates created their ideas. You can visit important historical buildings that are hundreds of years old. You can enjoy traditional Greek food at an outdoor restaurant and join the crowds in busy Syntagma Square.

RECOMMENDED

- Ancient architecture
- Traditional Greek food
- Relaxing day trips out of town

Hotel Fact File: Good cheap rooms. Many have balconies with views of this fabulous city.

Excursions: Day Trip to Poros $60
Spend a day exploring this peaceful island
Day Trip to Rafina $40
Eat and swim the day away in this quiet, coastal village
Acropolis Tour $25
An English-speaking guide will answer all your questions

6.3

The New York bike race

Aim	
To plan a route for a bike race in New York	
Language	
Prepositions of place and movement Directions	
Skills	
Speaking	
Lesson link	
Use after *Directions* SB p. 49	
Materials	
One copy of the criteria list worksheet and the map worksheet for each pair of students	

Pre-activity (5 minutes)

- Hold up a copy of the criteria worksheet. Ask students if they have been to a race like this, what the atmosphere is like, etc.

- Ask students to imagine they are the race organizers. Brainstorm what is involved in organizing a cycle race, e.g., spectator areas, TV crews, etc. Encourage students also to consider the practical issues of holding a race in the middle of a city, e.g., diverting traffic, food and toilet facilities, etc.

- Spend a few minutes reviewing prepositions of location, e.g., *across from*, *next to*, *between*, *behind*, etc., and prepositions of movement, e.g., *past*, *across*, *under*, etc., with the class.

Procedure (25 minutes)

- Explain that students are going to plan a route for a bike race in the middle of New York City.

- Divide students into pairs. Give each pair a copy of the map worksheet and the criteria for the race worksheet. Give students time to read through them and to check any items of vocabulary.

- In pairs, students work together to plan the route. Go around the room monitoring progress.

- When students have decided on their route, they present their route to another pair. Encourage them to use prepositions of location as they describe the route of the race in relation to the tourist attractions. Go around the room listening, correcting, and helping as necessary.

- Review as a class to see how everybody has interpreted the assignment.

Extension (10 minutes)

- Play a directions game using the map of New York City. Working in pairs, students take turns describing a route around New York for their partner to follow, e.g., *Go across the Brooklyn Bridge. Turn right on Broadway. Go up Broadway to 8th Street*, etc.

THE NEW YORK BIKE RACE

CRITERIA FOR RACE

1. Decide how long the race will be.

2. Start and finish the race in Brooklyn or Queens.

3. Include as many tourist attractions as possible.

4. Include long, straight runs for speed.

5. Include some parks for variety.

6. Decide where the support team will be.

7. Say where the TV cameras will be placed.

8. Say where the main spectator areas will be.

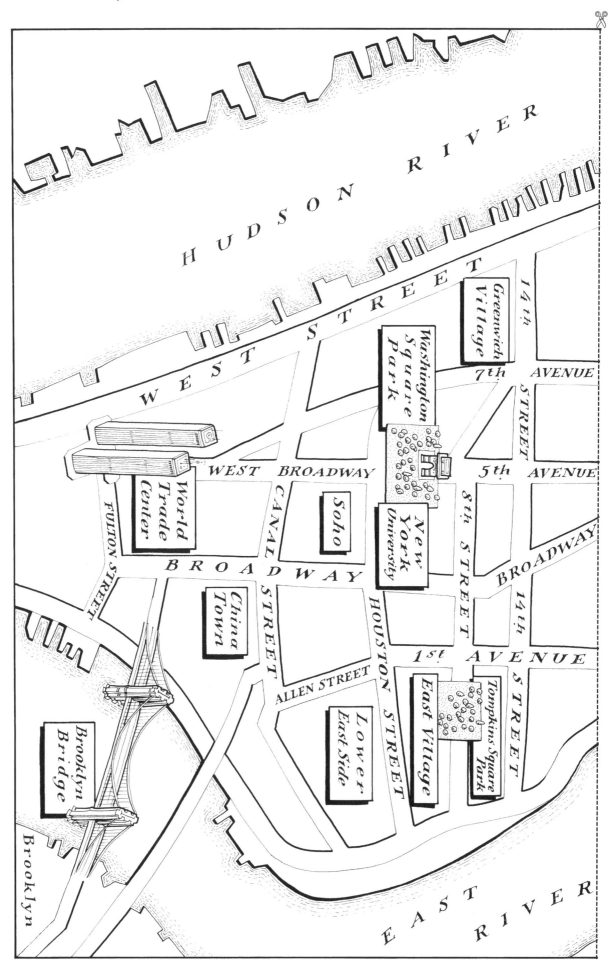

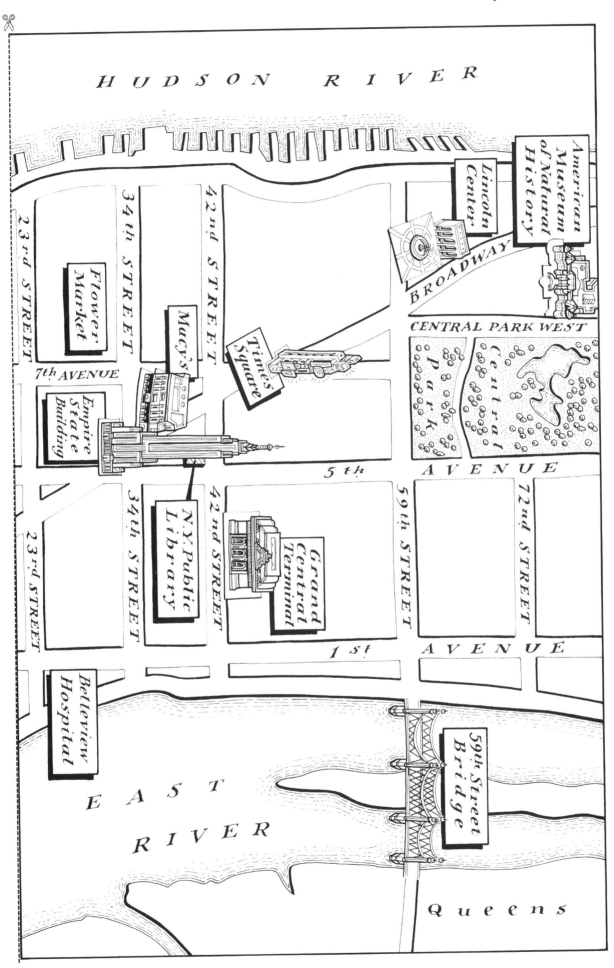

7.1

The People's Biography

Pre-activity (10 minutes)

- Ask students to tell you what they know about the native tribes of the Amazon. Write their ideas on the board.

- Ask students to imagine that they are going to interview some of these people to find out more about them. In pairs, students think of questions they would like to ask them.

- Review students' ideas as a class. Write some of the questions on the board.

Procedure (20 minutes)

- Explain that students are going to interview each other about their daily lives for a book called *The People's Biography*.

- Give each student a copy of the worksheet. Read through the note from the publisher and the back cover of the book with the class. Explain any unfamiliar vocabulary.

- Look at all the points covered in the back cover again with the class and ask students to think of questions they will need to ask to get all this information. Brainstorm a few ideas with the class.

- Individually, students think of more questions to ask. Go around the room helping as necessary.

- Divide students into pairs. Students take turns being the journalist and interviewing their partner, writing the answers in their notebooks. Go around the room listening, helping, and correcting as necessary.

Extension (10 minutes)

- Students write the entry for their partner for *The People's Biography* using the notes they made. Go around the room helping as necessary.

- You may want to display the entries on the classroom wall and allow students time to read each other's work.

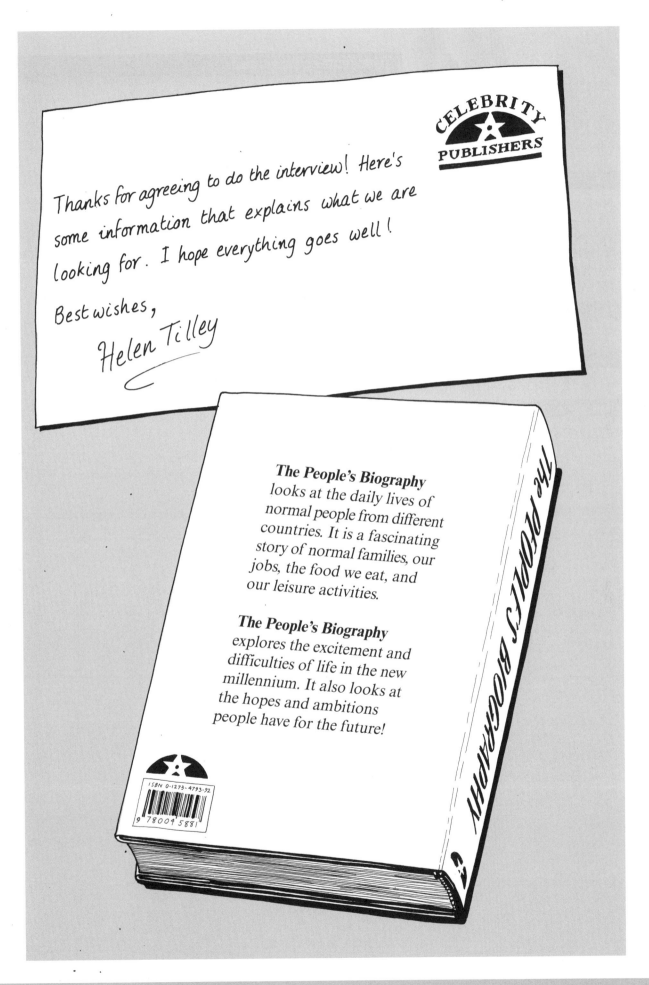

7.2

Aim

To read about different eras of twentieth-century music and talk about the significance of certain facts

Language

Past Tenses

Skills

Reading and Speaking

Lesson link

Use after *The band Style* SB p. 53

Materials

One copy of the music quiz worksheet and the twentieth-century music worksheet for each pair of students

Answers to the Quiz

1. Two   2. Jerry Lee Lewis   3. Mick Jagger, Keith Richards, Ronnie Wood, Charlie Watts   4. The Beatles   5. Sweden
6. The Beach Boys   7. 1982
8. Live Aid   9. Puerto Rico
10. Robbie Williams

love/glove	hate/wait
skin/pin	time/crime
feel/real	shame/fame
day/say	boy/toy
night/fight	hair/care
hour/power	eyes/lies
shock/clock	bar/car
stress/dress	kiss/miss

Pre-activity (15 minutes)

- Discuss different types of music in the twentieth century with the class. Make a list on the board, e.g., *Rock 'n' Roll, Punk, Heavy Metal, Dance*, etc. Encourage students to tell you the rock stars/bands which are/were famous in each category.

- Divide students into pairs. Hand out the music quiz worksheets for students to answer.

- Check the answers with the class.

Procedure (20 minutes)

- Explain that students are going to read about different eras of twentieth-century music and then, in pairs, discuss the significance of various facts.

- Divide students into pairs. Give Students A worksheet A, and Students B worksheet B.

- Individually, students read about their two eras of music. Go around the room explaining any unfamiliar vocabulary.

- In pairs, students take turns asking and answering questions about the six facts. Go around the room listening and helping as necessary.

- Review answers as a class. Ask students to tell you the significance of each fact.

Extension (20 minutes)

Suggested answers

A 1. They were the first punk rock band.
   2. David Bowie was a glam rock star.
   3. It was the biggest-selling album of all time.
   4. Glam rock stars wore makeup and colorful costumes.
   5. Tupac Shakur was a famous rapper.
   6. A lot of people went to raves to take drugs.

B 1. Elvis Presley sang rock 'n' roll songs.
   2. The Beatles started to perform in 1962.
   3. The Beatles were from Liverpool.
   4. In the 1960s this was the motto of the hippies.
   5. Bob Dylan's song, "Blowing in the Wind," was against nuclear weapons.
   6. Woodstock, the music festival, was in 1969.

- Write the rhyming word pairs on the left on the board:

- Working in small groups, students write one or two verses of a song. They should decide what kind of song they want to write, e.g., Rock 'n' roll, etc. Their task is to include as many of the rhyming words as possible.

Music quiz

20ᵀᴴ CENTURY MUSIC QUIZ

– 1950s –

1. How many Everly Brothers were there?
2. Who sang "Great Balls of Fire" in 1957?

– 1960s –

3. Name two members of the Rolling Stones.
4. Which famous band did Brian Epstein manage?

– 1970s –

5. Which country did ABBA come from?
6. Which band had a hit with "Surfing USA"?

– 1980s –

7. When did Madonna release her first song?
8. What was the name of the 1985 charity rock concerts in Britain and the United States?

– 1990s –

9. Where was Ricky Martin born?
10. Who started a solo career with the album, *Life thru a Lens*?

A Twentieth-century music

Rock 'n' Roll

Elvis Presley

When Elvis Presley started to play music in the mid-1950s he was very popular. Teenagers in America and Britain loved his rock 'n' roll music. This new type of music came from the rhythm and blues music that many black musicians played in America.

The USA was the main place for rock music (often called "pop music") until 1962 when four musicians from Liverpool started to perform. They were the Beatles, and they created a new type of rock 'n' roll called the "Mersey sound." The name comes from the river Mersey in Liverpool. The Beatles became one of the most successful bands of all time.

The Beatles

Flower Power

Bob Dylan

During the 1960s, some young people became unhappy with what the older generation was doing to the world. They were called "hippies" and they wore flowers to show that they were peaceful people. Their motto was "Make love, not war."

Their peaceful philosophy is in Bob Dylan's song, "Blowing in the Wind," which says that nuclear power is bad for the world.

In 1969, 500,000 hippies went to a music festival in an American town called Woodstock. For a long time this was the biggest-ever music festival.

Woodstock

Why are these things important to the history of rock music? Ask your partner.

1. The Sex Pistols
2. David Bowie
3. The album, *Thriller*

4. Makeup and colorful costumes
5. Tupac Shakur
6. Drugs

B Twentieth-century music

Glam to Punk Rock

In the early 1970s, a new generation of musicians arrived. They wanted to shock people and their music was called "Glam rock." Artists such as David Bowie wore colorful costumes and makeup.

In the mid-1970s, the desire to shock went further when a band called the Sex Pistols arrived. Their type of music was called "Punk Rock." The Sex Pistols had lots of fans. They were called "Punk Rockers" and they wore strange hairstyles, ripped jeans, and safety pins in their clothes.

David Bowie as Ziggy Stardust

The Rave Generation

A rave

In the 1990s, "rave" parties became popular. These are parties with hundreds of young people. They were illegal because a lot of people went to take drugs.

The 1990s was a time for mega-stars like Madonna and Michael Jackson. They sold more records than anybody else, and Michael Jackson made the biggest-selling album of all time, *Thriller*.

The end of the 1990s was a time when lots of different bands were popular. There were also lots of different styles of music, such as "Rap" where musicians speak the lyrics against a very strong rhythm. Tupac Shakur was a famous rapper.

Tupac Shakur

Why are these things important to the history of rock music? Ask your partner.

1. Elvis Presley
2. 1962
3. Liverpool
4. "Make love, not war"
5. Nuclear weapons
6. 1969

8.1

Baker's dozen

Aim

To define jobs to complete a crossword puzzle

Language

have to

Job vocabulary

Skills

Speaking

Lesson link

Use after *Jobs* SB p. 59

Materials

One copy of the worksheet cut in half for each pair of students

Pre-activity (5 minutes)

- Play a job guessing game with the class. Describe a job for students to guess, e.g., *This person has to work outside all day. He/She looks after animals* (farmer).

- Ask individual students to describe a job for the class to guess.

Procedure (15 minutes)

- Explain that students are going to work in pairs to complete a job crossword puzzle. Students are going to take turns giving definitions to their partner. Explain the significance of the activity title (a *baker's dozen* means *thirteen*). (This was the way bakers supplied bread in the past. They always added an extra loaf because there were big fines to pay if they were found to be supplying bread under an agreed weight.) Tell students that the activity is called *Baker's dozen* because there is a thirteenth secret job. The aim is to complete the other jobs to find out what it is. The letters making up the thirteenth job are in the shaded boxes.

- Divide students into pairs. Give Students A crossword A, and Students B crossword B. Tell them not to show each other their crosswords.

- Allow students time to prepare their definitions. Encourage students to define their jobs as clearly as possible to help their partner complete the blanks. Go around the room helping with vocabulary as necessary. You may want to pair Students A and Students B during this preparation stage.

- Students work in pairs to complete the crossword and then try to figure out the mystery job (*receptionist*).

- Review the answers as a class.

Extension (10 minutes)

- Play *Twenty questions* with the class. Think of a job, e.g., *dentist*. Students can ask you a maximum of 20 questions to try to guess the job, e.g., *Do you work inside? Do you earn a lot of money? Do you have to wear a uniform?* You can only answer *Yes* or *No*.

A Baker's dozen

Mystery job _____

✂ ---

B Baker's dozen

Mystery job _____

8.2

Chain card compound

Aim
To play dominoes to make compound nouns

Language
Compound nouns

Skills
Speaking

Lesson link
Use after *Words that go together* SB p. 64

Materials
Half the worksheet cut up for each group of students

Pre-activity (5 minutes)

- Play a compound noun game. Divide the class into groups of four students. Call out words, e.g., *book, hair, ice*, etc., and ask groups to say a compound noun, e.g., *bookcase, hair dryer, ice cream*, etc. Call out a maximum of ten words.

Procedure (15 minutes)

- Explain that students are going to place domino pieces which make compound nouns in such a way as to make a complete circle.
- Divide students into groups of four. Give each group a set of dominoes, either A or B.
- In their groups, students work cooperatively to make a complete circle. Go around the room monitoring and helping as necessary.
- When the circles are completed, groups check each other's circles.
- Review answers as a class.

Answers

A alarm clock, hair dryer, can opener, ice cream, earring, timetable, bookcase, tape recorder, traffic lights, rush hour

B bulletin board, sunset, train station, credit card, movie star, screwdriver, cigarette lighter, coffee break, earthquake, raincoat

Extension (10 minutes)

- Students use their circle of cards to make up a story. They should try to include all of the compound nouns in their story. Go around the room helping as necessary.
- Invite groups to tell their story to the class.

A

hour	alarm	clock	hair
dryer	can	opener	ice
cream	ear	ring	time
table	book	case	tape
recorder	traffic	lights	rush

B

coat	bulletin	board	sun
set	train	station	credit
card	movie	star	screw
driver	cigarette	lighter	coffee
break	earth	quake	rain

9.1

Hot verb 4-squares

Pre-activity (5 minutes)

- Write the following verb phrases on the board: *take someone out for dinner, get into trouble, do someone a favor, make someone angry*. Ask students to think of the last time they did these things and to tell the class about it.

Procedure (20 minutes)

- Explain that students are going to play a game where the aim is to get a line (vertical, horizontal, or diagonal) of four squares. In each square is a verb (*take*, *get*, *do*, or *make*). Students take turns picking up a phrase card and deciding which verb it can be used with, e.g., *into trouble* can be used with *get*. Students then have to make a sentence with the verb phrase to get that square, e.g., *I got into trouble because I didn't do my homework*. You may want to demonstrate the game with a student to make sure everyone understands.

- Divide students into pairs. Give each pair a copy of the *Hot verb 4-squares* board game and a set of the phrase cards.

- Students place the phrase cards face down, then take turns picking up a phrase card and playing the game. When students make a correct sentence, they should write their name on that square. Encourage students to stop their opponent from making a line of four by blocking. Go around monitoring and correcting as necessary.

  Note: There are eight phrases for each verb. In some cases a phrase can collocate with more than one verb, e.g., *get a birthday card, make a birthday card*. Clearly this is acceptable. However, tell your students that you are the referee if students cannot agree among themselves.

- Review answers as a class. Call out a phrase and have students call out the verb.

Extension (10 minutes)

- Students write a short account of one of the situations they discussed during the game. Go around the room helping with vocabulary as necessary. Invite several students to read their accounts to the class.

Phrase cards

a birthday card	a new car	a complaint	a job
a mistake	a phone call	a photograph	a shower
angry	your homework	care	friends with someone
into trouble	me a favor	your best	off the bus
along with someone	out of a car	part in a race	someone's advice
some shopping	someone a drink	someone angry	someone out for dinner
sure	the laundry	dinner	the dog for a walk
the housework	the dishes	two tablets a day	up your mind

T A K E	**G E T**	**M A K E**	**D O**
D O	**M A K E**	**G E T**	**T A K E**
G E T	**D O**	**T A K E**	**M A K E**
M A K E	**T A K E**	**D O**	**G E T**
T A K E	**G E T**	**M A K E**	**D O**
D O	**M A K E**	**G E T**	**T A K E**
G E T	**D O**	**T A K E**	**M A K E**
M A K E	**T A K E**	**D O**	**G E T**

T A K E	**G E T**	**M A K E**	**D O**
D O	**M A K E**	**G E T**	**T A K E**
G E T	**D O**	**T A K E**	**M A K E**
M A K E	**T A K E**	**D O**	**G E T**
T A K E	**G E T**	**M A K E**	**D O**
D O	**M A K E**	**G E T**	**T A K E**
G E T	**D O**	**T A K E**	**M A K E**
M A K E	**T A K E**	**D O**	**G E T**

9.2

Aim
A board game to role-play hotel situations

Language
Reserve a hotel room, asking for information, and making requests
Fluency practice

Skills
Speaking

Lesson link
Use after *In a hotel* SB pp. 72–73

Materials
One copy of the worksheet for each group of four students

Pre-activity (5 minutes)

- Discuss hotels with the class. Ask students to tell you about any experiences, good or bad, they have had while staying in a hotel.

Procedure (25 minutes)

- Explain that this is a mini role-play activity played as a board game. Students play in pairs and move around the board using a counter. They flip a coin to move (heads = move one square, tails = move two squares). Each square presents students with a situation where they play the role of a customer. In each case, one student plays the role of a guest and the other the role of a hotel receptionist. The receptionist will need to refer to the "Hotel Headway" information sheet in the center of the board.

- Divide students into groups of four and give each group a copy of the worksheet. Give them time to read through it and to check any items of vocabulary. Use this time to brainstorm phrases and vocabulary students think they may need e.g., *How can I help you? Can I . . . , I'd like . . . , Could I . . . , I'm not happy with . . .* , etc. Ask each student to choose a "marker," e.g., a coin, paper clip, etc., to move around the board.

- Students play the game. Go around the room listening and helping with vocabulary as necessary. Do not correct students while they are playing but make a note of common errors to go over with the whole class at the end.

Extension (10 minutes)

- In pairs, students choose one of the squares on the board where they had to go back a square, e.g., *The bed sheets are dirty*. They role-play a situation where they make a complaint. Go around the room listening and helping and correcting as necessary.

- Invite several pairs to act out their dialogue for the class.

Start

Finish

1 Book a room for three nights. Find out how much it costs. Ask if breakfast is included. ▶

2 There are no rooms available! Go back one square. ◀

3 Ask the receptionist to arrange a wake-up call for tomorrow. ▼

15 It is time to go home. Pay your bill. ▲

4 Your room is beautiful, but the shower doesn't work. Tell the receptionist. ▼

14 There is a large spider in the bathtub! Go back one square. ▼

5 The food is terrible! Go back one square. ▲

13 You need to go to the airport. Ask the receptionist to order a taxi. ▲

6 Your room is terrible! Demand a new room immediately. ▼

12 The hotel restaurant looks good! Reserve a table for tonight. ▲

7 You need to relax. Ask the receptionist about the hotel facilities. ▼

11 The bed sheets are dirty! Go back one square. ▶

10 Ask the receptionist if there is any entertainment today. ◀

9 You are hungry now. Telephone room service and order some food. ◀

8 The swimming pool is closed! Go back one square. ▲

HOTEL HEADWAY
A warm welcome every time!

50 Luxurious Rooms

SINGLE	$90.00 per night
DOUBLE	$155.00 per night

Price includes breakfast (served between 7 A.M. and 9 A.M.)

... and much more!

- INDOOR SWIMMING POOL
- SAUNA AND WHIRLPOOL
- 9-HOLE GOLF COURSE

PLUS our famous restaurant TASTE BUDS

(BOOK A TABLE AT RECEPTION)

Room service available

"**Snack bar**" ... tea or coffee and snacks $5.50

"**Light lunch**" ... your choice of sandwich and a glass of soda or mineral water $7.75

"**Extravaganza**" ... smoked salmon and champagne $15.95

Today's entertainment

1 P.M.—**Bus tour to the historic Widdling Village** (tickets $10)

9 P.M.—**Music in the lounge**
Olde Spice and the Wailers
—as seen on TV!

10.1

The last time you felt . . .

Aim

A free-speaking activity based upon feelings

Language

Adjectives
Present and past tenses

Skills

Speaking

Lesson link

Use after -ed / -ing adjectives SB p. 77

Materials

One copy of the worksheet for each student with the conversation cards cut out

Pre-activity (10 minutes)

- Divide students into groups of three to five. Hand out the adjectives and prompts portion of the worksheet to each student. Discuss what feeling each of the pictures represents.

- In their groups, students discuss what feeling goes with each prompt. Give them an example structure to use, e.g., *You feel sick when you have a cold.* Review answers as a class.

> **Suggested answers**
>
> 1. bored 2. tired 3. sick 4. confused 5. optimistic 6. angry
> 7. under pressure 8. excited 9. nervous 10. afraid 11. sad 12. worried
> 13. very happy 14. pessimistic

Procedure (20 minutes)

- Give each student a set of conversation cards. Individually students think about a real feeling they had for the time references on the cards, e.g., *Last week I was nervous because it was the first day of school.* Then they write the adjective on the card (nothing more).

  Note: Talking about feelings is often a very good way to bring students closer together. However, make it clear at the beginning that students should only write down feelings that they can talk about openly and comfortably.

- Divide students into pairs. Students exchange conversation cards and take turns asking and answering about the feelings, e.g., *Why did you feel happy last year? I felt happy because my sister had a baby.* The listening student can help by asking more questions, e.g., *What is the baby's name? What day was she born?* etc. Go around the room listening and helping as necessary.

Extension (10 minutes)

- Students write about one of the experiences they discussed. Go around the room helping as necessary.

How do you feel . . .

1. when you have nothing to do or something is not interesting?
2. when it is late?
3. when you have a cold?
4. when you don't understand something?
5. when you feel good about the future?
6. when you are annoyed?
7. when you have too much to do?
8. when you are enthusiastic about something?
9. when you must do something that is difficult and important?
10. when you are frightened?
11. when you cry?
12. when a person you love is late and hasn't telephoned?
13. when you pass a test?
14. when you feel negative about the future?

sad

afraid

nervous

tired

angry   worried

bored

sick

very happy

under pressure

confused

optimistic

pessimistic

excited

Conversation cards

now	today

yesterday	last week

last year	when I was a child

10.2

Aim

To check information in four eyewitness accounts to find the true story

Language

Asking for and giving information

Past tenses

Skills

Reading and Speaking

Lesson link

Use after *Into the wild* SB pp. 78–79

Materials

One copy of the artist's impression worksheet and one copy of the eyewitness account worksheets for each group of four students

Answers

A **blue** sports car came down Side Street at approximately **8:30** at night. It was getting dark and the streetlights were on. The car's headlights **were not on.** The driver of the car was a man. **He was in his twenties** and he had brown hair.

As the sports car approached the intersection with Main Street, the traffic light facing it turned green and the car kept going. Main Street is a one-way street so the sports car should have turned right. However, the sports car **turned left** instead. He was going around **60–70 km an hour**. The driver of the sports car didn't see the bus that was coming down Main Street until the last minute because **he was talking on his cell phone.**

Luckily, the bus swerved out of the way, but it crashed into the bus shelter. There were some people waiting at the shelter but they got out of the way!

The sports car didn't stop. The police are now looking for the driver. The car's license plate number is **305 PWA.**

Pre-activity (5 minutes)

- Discuss traffic accidents with the class. Ask students to tell you the most common causes of accidents, e.g., *speeding, drinking, not paying enough attention, talking on cell phones,* etc. Do students think that people should be allowed to use a cell phone when driving? Why/Why not?

Procedure (25 minutes)

- Explain that students are police investigators and each has an eyewitness account of a traffic accident. Some accounts contain inaccuracies and their task is to find the correct version of events according to the majority consensus.

- Divide students into groups of four and give each group a copy of the artist's impression of the scene of the accident. Ask them to discuss what they think has happened. Review ideas as a class.

- Then give each member of each group a different eyewitness account: A, B, C, or D. Give students time to read through them and to check any items of vocabulary. Tell them there are eight facts to discuss with the other police investigators.

- Students take turns asking the other members of their group questions to check the information in their own account, e.g., *What color was the car? How old was the man? What time did the accident happen?* etc. Go around the room listening and helping as necessary.

- Review answers as a class. Did students find the eight facts?

Extension (5 minutes)

- Discuss with the class the punishment they think the man should receive for causing the accident.

Artist's impression

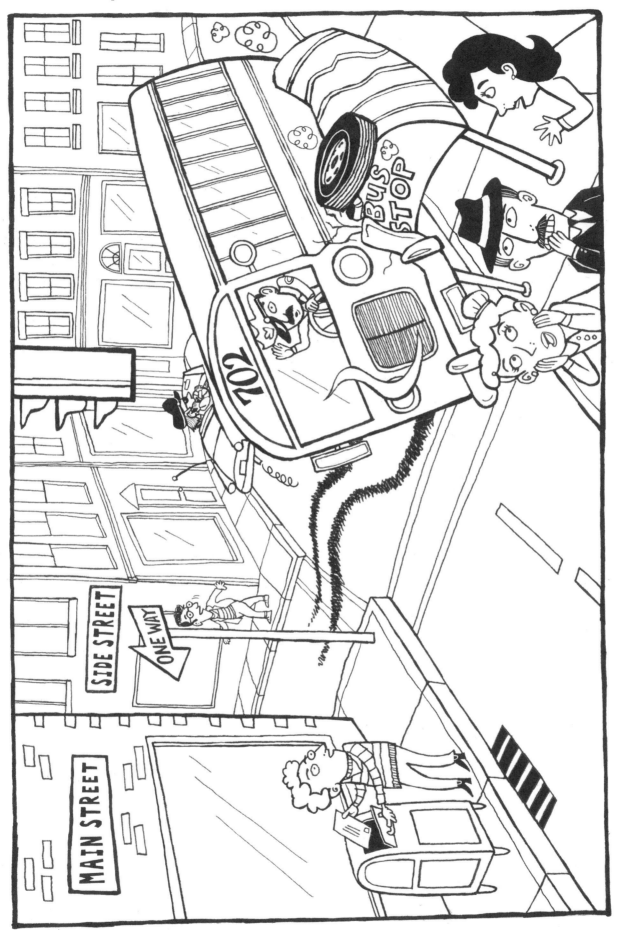

Eyewitness accounts

A

Mike Tiffany

I saw a sports car driving down Side Street at about 8:30 in the evening. It was getting dark, and the streetlights were on. The car's headlights were very bright, but I could see the car was blue. I also saw the driver ... a man in his twenties with brown hair.

As the sports car approached the intersection with Main Street, the traffic light facing it turned green and the car kept going. Main Street is a one-way street and the sports car should have turned right after turning the corner. However, the sports car turned left instead of right. He was going around 60–70 km an hour. The driver of the sports car didn't see a bus that was coming down Main Street, until the last minute because he was talking on his cell phone.

Luckily, the bus swerved out of the way, but it crashed into the bus shelter. There were some people waiting in the shelter, but they got out of the way!

I thought the sports car would stop after the accident, but it didn't! I saw the license plate number, though. It was 305 PUA.

B

Annette Rosie

I saw a blue sports car driving down Side Street at about 7:30 in the evening. It was getting dark, and the streetlights were on. However, the car's headlights were not on. I also saw the driver ... a man in his twenties with brown hair.

As the sports car approached the intersection with Main Street, the traffic light facing it turned green and the car kept going. Main Street is a one-way street and the sports car should have turned right after turning the corner. However, the sports car turned left instead of right. He was going around 30–40 km an hour. The driver of the sports car didn't see a bus that was coming down Main Street until the last minute because he was talking on his cell phone.

Luckily, the bus swerved out of the way, but it crashed into the bus shelter. There were some people waiting in the shelter, but they got out of the way!

I thought the sports car would stop after the accident, but it didn't! I saw the license plate number, though. It was 305 PWA.

C

John Vincent

I saw a purple sports car driving down Side Street at about 8:30 in the evening. It was getting dark, and the streetlights were on. However, the car's headlights were not on.
I also saw the driver ... a man in his twenties with brown hair.

The car approached the intersection with Main Street. The traffic light facing it turned green and the car kept going. Main Street is a one-way street and the sports car should have turned right after turning the corner. However, the sports car went straight instead of turning right. He was going around 60-70 km an hour. The driver of the sports car didn't see a bus that was coming down Main Street, until the last minute because he was talking on his cell phone.

Luckily, the bus swerved out of the way, but it crashed into the bus shelter. There were some people waiting in the bus shelter, but they got out of the way!

I thought the sports car would stop after the accident, but it didn't! I saw the license plate number, though. It was 305 PWA.

✂ --

D

Miriam Plumber

I saw a blue sports car driving down Side Street at about 8:30 in the evening. It was getting dark, and the streetlights were on. However, the car's headlights were not on.
I also saw the driver ... a man in his forties with brown hair.

As the sports car approached the intersection with Main Street, the traffic light facing it turned green and the car kept going. Main Street is a one-way street and the sports car should have turned right after turning the corner. However, the sports car turned left instead of right. He was going around 60-70 km an hour. The driver of the sports car didn't see a bus that was coming down Main Street until the last minute because he was eating a sandwich.

Luckily, the bus swerved out of the way, but it crashed into the bus shelter. There were some people waiting in the shelter, but they got out of the way!

I thought the sports car would stop after the accident, but it didn't! I saw the license plate number, though. It was 305 PWA.

11.1

The robbery

Aim
To tell a story using the past passive

Language
Past passive

Skills
Speaking

Lesson link
Use after *Active and passive* SB pp. 84–85

Materials
One copy of the worksheet for each pair of students

Pre-activity (5 minutes)

- Discuss bank robberies with the class. Ask students to tell you about any robberies they have heard of in the news or seen in movies. Brainstorm words associated with bank robberies, e.g., *safe, gun, hostages, arrested, security guard, masked men*, etc.

Procedure (20 minutes)

- Explain that students are going to tell the story of a bank robbery using pictures and captions as prompts.

- Divide students into pairs, and give each pair a copy of the worksheet.

- Students look at the pictures and work out the story. Then they reconstruct the story using the prompts. Students practice telling the story in pairs. Go around the room listening and correcting as necessary.

> **Answers**
> City Bank was robbed this morning by masked men.
> $1 million was taken.
> A security guard was tied up.
> The manager was told to open the safe.
> The manager was taken hostage.
> The manager was found in a field three hours later.
> A gun was found in a trash can.
> The gun was tested for fingerprints.
> One of the robbers was identified.
> The robbers were caught at home.

- Ask students to prepare to tell the story as a TV news report. Encourage students to make the report as authentic as possible.

- Invite several pairs to act out their news report in front of the class. You may want to make this a chain news report by stopping each student after one sentence and asking another student to continue the story.

Extension (10 minutes)

- Students write a newspaper article about the robbery. Go around the room helping with vocabulary as necessary.

THE ROBBERY

City Bank / rob / this morning / masked men

$1 million / take

security guard / tie up

manager / tell / open the safe

manager / take hostage

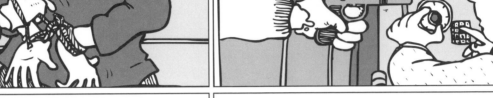

manager / find in a field / three hours later

gun / find in a trash can

gun / test for fingerprints

one of the robbers / identify

the robbers / catch / at home

11.2

When and Where?

Aim

A quiz to practice asking questions in the passive.

Language

Passives: present and past

Skills

Speaking

Lesson link

Use after *Active and passive* SB pp. 84–85

Materials

One copy of the worksheet cut in half for each pair of students

Pre-activity (5 minutes)

- Write this question and possible answers on the board: *When / the movie* Titanic */ make? a) 1996 b) 1997 c) 1998*. Ask students to tell you who was in the movie (Leonardo DiCaprio and Kate Winslet) and then tell you the question: *When was the movie* Titanic *made?* Now ask students to tell you the answer using the passive (The movie Titanic *was made in 1997*).

Procedure (20 minutes)

- Explain that students are going to ask each other general knowledge questions using the passive (present and past).

- Divide students into pairs. Give Students A worksheet A, and Students B worksheet B. Give students several minutes to read through them, to check any items of vocabulary, and to work out the questions. Point out that some questions will be in the present passive.

Questions

A
1. When was *Hamlet* written?
2. Where was Kennedy shot?
3. Where are oranges grown?
4. When was the CD invented?
5. Where was the first photograph taken?
6. Where is the most coffee grown?
7. When was the telephone invented?
8. When were the first cigarettes produced?
9. Where was Tutankhamen found?
10. When was the *Mona Lisa* painted?

B
1. When was the radio invented?
2. Where are NASA Space Shuttles launched?
3. Where was Elvis Presley buried?
4. When was Coca Cola invented?
5. Where is the most pollution from cars produced?
6. When was radioactivity discovered?
7. When was Tiger Woods born?
8. Where was John Lennon killed?
9. Where are the Crown Jewels kept?
10. When was the Great Wall of China built?

- In pairs, students take turns asking each other the questions and giving the three possible answers. (Tell students the correct answer is shown by the shading around the letter.) Students get a point for each correct answer. Go around the room listening and correcting as necessary.

- Review answers as a class. How many points did students score in the quiz?

Extension (10 minutes)

- Students write sentences about the questions they asked, e.g., Hamlet *was written in 1601*.

A

When and Where?

1. When / *Hamlet* / write? **a** 1601 **b** 1885 **c** 1975	**6.** Where / the most coffee / grow? **a** Mexico **b** Brazil **c** Kenya
2. Where / Kennedy / shoot? **a** New York **b** Washington **c** Dallas	**7.** When / the telephone / invent? **a** 1750 **b** 1878 **c** 1905
3. Where / oranges / grow? **a** Arizona **b** Florida **c** Washington	**8.** When / the first cigarettes / produce? **a** 17th century **b** 18th century **c** 19th century
4. When / the CD / invent? **a** 1979 **b** 1969 **c** 1959	**9.** Where / Tutankhamen / find? **a** Egypt **b** Thailand **c** Australia
5. Where / the first photograph / take? **a** France **b** Italy **c** Japan	**10.** When / the *Mona Lisa* / paint? **a** 1903 **b** 1726 **c** 1540?

- -

B

When and Where?

1. When / the radio / invent? **a** 1745 **b** 1895 **c** 1901	**6.** When / radioactivity / discover? **a** 1426 **b** 1898 **c** 1944
2. Where / NASA Space Shuttles / launch? **a** Cape Canaveral **b** Fort Lauderdale **c** Houston	**7.** When / Tiger Woods / born? **a** 1970 **b** 1972 **c** 1975
3. Where / Elvis Presley / bury? **a** Heartbreak Hotel **b** The White House **c** Graceland	**8.** Where / John Lennon / kill? **a** New York **b** Liverpool **c** Paris
4. When / Coca Cola / invent? **a** 1908 **b** 1945 **c** 1886	**9.** Where / the Crown Jewels / keep? **a** The Tower of London **b** Buckingham Palace **c** 10 Downing Street
5. Where / the most pollution from cars / produce? **a** Europe **b** USA **c** China	**10.** When / the Great Wall of China / build? **a** 600 B.C. **b** 400 B.C. **c** 200 B.C.

12.1

Problem Doctor

Pre-activity (5 minutes)

- Set the scene. Ask students where they can go if they have a physical problem (doctor, hospital), and if they have a mental problem (psychiatrist). Then ask students where they can go for everyday problems and dilemmas (friend, advice column). Ask students what problems advice columns generally deal with (relationships).

Procedure (25 minutes)

- Explain that students are writing an advice column called "Problem Doctor" and it is their job to give people advice about everyday problems.

- Divide students into groups of six to eight. Then divide each group in half, A and B. Students A are "Problem Doctor." Ask them to set up their "offices" in different corners of the room. Students B have the problems. Give Students B each a role card. Their task is to get advice from each doctor and to write it in their notebooks. They have five minutes to visit each doctor in their group.

- When Students B have visited all the doctors in their group, the roles are reversed. This time Students B are doctors and Students A are patients.

- Review answers as a class. Ask each student to explain what their problem was and to say what advice was given to them. The different pieces of advice can vary enormously, often with humorous results!

Extension (10 minutes)

- Students write a letter to an advice column and the reply based on the problem and the advice they were given. Go around the room monitoring and helping with vocabulary as necessary.

Last week you stole some money from your best friend. It was a crazy thing to do, but you really needed the money. Now you feel bad, but you don't want to say anything and risk losing his friendship.

**If you were me,
what would you do?**

You have forgotten your wife's/husband's birthday! You can see she/he is waiting for a big surprise!

**If you were me,
what would you do?**

Last week you saw a car hit a cyclist in the street, but the driver didn't stop. The accident happened very quickly, but you saw the driver. It was your best friend!

**If you were me,
what would you do?**

Last night you saw your friend's husband in a restaurant. He was having a romantic dinner ... with another woman!

**If you were me,
what would you do?**

Your brother always has money problems. You have helped him in the past, but he rarely pays you back. Yesterday he asked if he could borrow $1,500. "It's really important this time!" he said.

**If you were me,
what would you do?**

The man next door always plays loud music. You have told him many times that it is a problem, but he never listens.

**If you were me,
what would you do?**

You work in a bookstore where the pay is terrible. It's your friend's birthday, but you have no money to buy a present. She loves reading ... and there are lots of books around you.

**If you were me,
what would you do?**

You work with a woman who always takes your good ideas and says they are hers! But there is another problem ... she is the daughter of your boss.

**If you were me,
what would you do?**

12.2

Aim
To practice the Second Conditional

Language
Second Conditional
Fluency practice

Skills
Speaking

Lesson link
Use after *What would you do?* SB p. 92

Materials
Copies of the worksheet cut up allowing each student at least one card at any one time

Pre-activity (5 minutes)

- Write the following question on the board: *What would you do if I cancelled class tomorrow with no warning?* Ask your students what they would do.

Procedure (20 minutes)

- Explain that students are going to interview each other about what they would do in a hypothetical situation. Because the situations are hypothetical, remind students they have to use the Second Conditional, i.e., *What would you do if …?*

- Ask students to join you in the center of the room. Give each student a rolecard. Students interview each other to find out what they would do in the situation. Then they go back to their desk and write a short sentence about that person, e.g., *If Paula found a gold watch in the street, she would keep it!* Go around the room listening and making sure students use the Second Conditional and conjugate the verbs correctly.

- Then students exchange their old card for a new one. The game continues until everybody has written at least three sentences.

- Review answers as a class. Talk through the situations and encourage students to say what their classmates would do.

Extension (10 minutes)

- Students use one of the situations they were asked about and imagine that it actually happened. They write a short account of what happened and what they did. Go around the room helping as necessary.

- Invite several students to read their accounts to the class.

you see a ghost	you win the lottery
you see a lion in the street	a friend asks to borrow $1,000
you are offered a great job in another country	you find a gold watch in the street
your best friend steals something	you lose all your money on vacation
you have an argument with your parents	your son/daughter starts smoking
a sales assistant gives you too much change	a waiter in a restaurant is rude to you
you borrow (and lose) a CD from your friend	you crash your dad's car
you accidently break someone's window (they are not home)	you see your best friend's husband with another woman
you find out that a friend has lied to you	you forget to meet someone
someone gives you the answers to an exam	you forget your mother's birthday

13.1

Aim
To role-play a first day at college

Language
Fluency practice

Skills
Speaking

Lesson link
Use after *Street life* SB pp. 98–99

Materials
One copy of the worksheet cut up for each group of four students

Pre-activity (5 minutes)

- Discuss starting college with the class. Ask students, in pairs, to discuss what questions they would want to ask people who were starting college at the same time as them. Review ideas as a class.

- Explain that in the United States people often go to college in a different city and students make friends with people from very different backgrounds.

Procedure (20 minutes)

- Explain that students are going to take on the role of somebody who has just arrived at a college in a new town. Students are going to mingle with their new friends and speak to each other in order to find things they have in common.

- Divide students into groups of four and give each student a rolecard: **A**, **B**, **C**, or **D**.

- Students hold a conversation with each member of the group and ask questions to find things they have in common, e.g., *Where are you from? What is your major? What sports do you do? What do you like doing in the evening? What did you do last year? Why did you choose this college?* When they have found something in common with someone else, they write that person's name in the blank box on their rolecards. Then they move on to the next person.

- When everybody has finished, ask students to share what they discussed to find out what they have in common with each other.

Extension (10 minutes)

- Students write a letter home talking about their new friends and describing the things they have in common. Go around the room helping with vocabulary as necessary.

A ▼ Jim ▼

Hometown:	Chicago	
Major:	Biology	
Sport:	Table tennis	
Evening activity:	Cafes and clubs	
Last year:	In high school	
Why this college:	Good nightlife	

B ▼ Mike ▼

Hometown:	Dallas	
Major:	Biology	
Sport:	Swimming	
Evening activity:	Cafes and clubs	
Last year:	Working	
Why this college:	Good sports facilities	

C ▼ Stephanie ▼

Hometown:	Dallas	
Major:	History	
Sport:	Table tennis	
Evening activity:	Movies and theater	
Last year:	Working	
Why this college:	Good nightlife	

D ▼ Gemma ▼

Hometown:	Chicago	
Major:	History	
Sport:	Swimming	
Evening activity:	Movies and theater	
Last year:	In high school	
Why this college:	Good sports facilities	

13.2

Aim

To choose the best person for a job

Language

Asking and answering questions

Tense review

Fluency practice

Skills

Speaking and Reading

Lesson link

Use after *A funny way to make a living*
SB pp. 102–103

Materials

Two copies of the job description and interview notes cut up for each group of four students

Pre-activity (5 minutes)

- Discuss different jobs with the class. Ask students what attributes/skills people need to do different jobs, e.g., a teacher (*patience, enjoy working with students,* etc.).

Procedure (20 minutes)

- Explain that students work for a recruitment agency which interviews job candidates for clients. Their task is to choose the best person for the job of tour guide. Each candidate has some relevant experience or qualifications, but nobody is the obvious choice.

- Divide students into groups of four and give each group two copies of the job description. Students read the form. Explain any unfamiliar vocabulary.

- Then give each member of the group one of the interview notes: A, B, C, or D. Give students time to read through them and to check any items of vocabulary.

- Students then take turns presenting their candidate to the rest of the group. The group discusses the strong and weak points of each candidate and agree who should get the job. Go around the room listening and helping as necessary.

- Review answers as a class. Ask groups who they chose and why.

Extension (10 minutes)

- In their groups, students write a short report explaining why they have chosen a certain person for the job of tour guide. They should highlight this person's strengths but also draw attention to possible weaknesses. Go around the room helping as necessary.

Job description

Banks Recruitment Consultants

Job title: **TOUR GUIDE**

Main responsibilities: Taking groups of people on vacation to tourist destinations

Qualifications: One or two years' work experience. But would consider a college graduate with a degree in Tourism.
Languages a big advantage.

Personality:
- Somebody who gets along very well with people
- Leadership skills
- Ability to find solutions in difficult situations
- Creative
- Somebody who wants to help people
- Honest

Appearance: Neat but casual

Interests:
- Travel
- Local culture and customs
- Somebody who likes to socialize
- Interest in food and drink
- Prepared to work evenings

Interview notes

A   ## John Miles

Worked in cafes in Acapulco and Rio de Janeiro

Speaks fluent Spanish and Portuguese

Before that he was a lifeguard in California

Traveled through Africa on a bike!

Likes theater and has directed plays

B   ## Hilary Stone

Has a college degree in Leisure and Tourism

Enjoys reading and movies

Worked in a customer service department for one year

Speaks fluent Korean, Chinese, and Spanish

Has two dogs and a rabbit

C   ## Sandra Nash

Studied Art History in college

Organized the college radio station

Speaks some Japanese

Likes to go to cafes and clubs

Has never traveled abroad

D   ## Norman Blarney

Has worked as a tour guide for five years

Has traveled all over the world

Speaks Japanese, Greek, and Thai

Interested in art, classical music, and architecture

14.1

Family feuds

Aim

To discuss a seating arrangement for a feuding family

Language

Fluency practice

Skills

Reading and Speaking

Lesson link

Use after *A love story* SB pp. 106–107

Materials

One copy of the worksheet cut up for each group of four students

Pre-activity (5 minutes)

- Discuss the problem of members of a family not getting along well with each other. Encourage students to recount stories from books or movies and to explain what the problem was. Were the situations ever resolved? How?

Procedure (20 minutes)

- Explain that students have to arrange a seating plan for a family meal. However, their choices are limited because everybody seems to be upset with everyone else.

- Divide students into pairs. Give Students A worksheet A, and Students B worksheet B. Give students time to read through them and to check any items of vocabulary.

- Put a pair A with a pair B. In their groups, students describe who hates who and why. Go around the room listening and helping as necessary.

- Then groups arrange a seating plan for the family dinner. They must try not to sit feuding family members next to each other.

- Review answers as a class. Who did students seat next to each other?

Extension (10 minutes)

- In pairs, students choose two people who are seated next to each other in their final seating plan. They make up a conversation between these two people where they talk about the other people in the family (especially the ones they hate the most!).

- Invite pairs of students to act out their conversation in front of the class.

A

AUNT MABEL *Age 80. Married to Henry Greece*

 Aunt Mabel hates her husband. The only reason she married him was because he has a lot of money.

 She also hates her sister, Aunt Hilda. When their parents died, Hilda inherited everything.

LYDIA O'DONNEL *Age 30. Married to Winston O'Donnel. Madeleine's stepmother*

 Lydia hates Martin because he always says terrible things about her husband.

 She also hates Henry. They have very different political ideas and never agree.

WINSTON O'DONNEL *Age 55. Married to Lydia. Madeleine's father*

 Winston hates his daughter, Madeleine, because she only contacts him when she wants something, usually money.

 He also hates Mara. She ran over his dog with her car last summer.

AUNT HILDA *Age 75. Aunt Mabel's sister*

 Aunt Hilda hates her sister, Mabel, because she didn't invite her to her wedding 50 years ago!

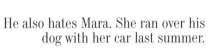 She also hates Jay because he doesn't work but spends a lot of the family money.

MADELEINE O'DONNEL *Age 29. Winston's daughter. Martin's girlfriend*

 She hates her stepmother, Lydia. Lydia is too young to be married to Madeleine's father!

 She also hates Cousin Jay because he was always mean to her when they were children.

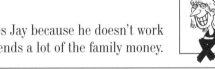

B

MARTIN HOWARD *Age 30. Madeleine's boyfriend*

Martin hates Roger Blueberry. Two years ago they had a successful business together until Roger left and took half the money!

He also hates Winston because he has never accepted him as a member of the family.

MARA BLUEBERRY *Age 55. Roger's ex-wife*

Mara hates her ex-husband, Roger. She only comes to these family dinners to stay friendly with Henry—and his money!

She also hates Winston O'Donnel. He once asked her to marry him, then changed his mind.

HENRY GREECE *Age 82. Aunt Mabel's husband*

Henry has always hated his wife because she gossips to everyone about him.

He also hates Lydia. She once said he was "an unfriendly, stupid, old man" in front of everybody.

ROGER BLUEBERRY *Age 58. Mara's ex-husband*

Roger hates his ex-wife, Mara, because she ignores him completely. She only comes to these dinners because she wants Henry's money!

He also hates Madeleine. She once told the local newspaper that he was dishonest. He lost a lot of customers after that story!

COUSIN JAY *Age 27. Aunt Hilda's nephew*

Jay hates Martin. Ten years ago Martin said he had the answers for a school test. They were all wrong and Jay failed!

He also hates Aunt Hilda. When he didn't get into college she stopped paying him $1,000 every month!

14.2

The good-bye game

Aim

To role-play saying good-bye in a variety of situations (formal and informal)

Language

Fluency practice

Skills

Speaking

Lesson link

Use at the end of Unit 14

Materials

One copy of the worksheet cut up for each class of 16 students

Pre-activity (5 minutes)

- Discuss formal and informal situations with the class. Who do they talk to in a formal/informal manner? How do they change the way they speak according to the situation?

Procedure (30 minutes)

- Explain that students are going to prepare and act out a short conversation in which different people say good-bye. Brainstorm expressions people use when they are saying good-bye, e.g., *Good-bye, Have a safe trip. Have a good weekend. Good luck,* etc.

- Divide students into pairs. Hand out a different situation card to each pair.

- In pairs, students read the card and then write a mini-dialogue between the two characters on their card. Explain that they are going to act out the dialogue. Give students time to practice the dialogue. Go around the room helping as necessary.

- Write the following situations on the board:
  A mother and her son at the airport
  Two colleagues at work on a Friday afternoon
  A teacher and a student at the end of the school year
  Two prisoners
  An airport official and a passenger
  Two spies on an enemy border
  A woman and her elderly father
  Two students at the end of the school year

- Ask each pair to act out their dialogue. The task of the rest of the class is to follow the dialogue and to try and guess which situation on the board is being enacted.

- Have the class vote to choose the best dialogue.

Extension (10 minutes)

- Students think of new situations and act out a new dialogue. Go around the room listening and helping as necessary.

- Invite pairs to act out their new dialogues for the class.

A mother and her son at the airport

The son is leaving to travel around the world. She is worried, and wants to make sure he hasn t forgotten anything. The son is excited and wants to start his trip as soon as possible!

Two colleagues at work on a Friday afternoon

One person is going on vacation for two weeks. The other colleague hopes he/she will have a good time, but he/she is also jealous.

A teacher and a student at the end of the school year

The teacher asks the student what he/she is doing during summer vacation. The student doesn t like the teacher and can t wait to leave the school.

Two prisoners

One prisoner is leaving after 25 years. He plans to really enjoy his new freedom! The other prisoner is sad to see his friend leaving.

An airport official and a passenger

The airport official asks the passenger for his ticket and passport. The passenger asks what gate his flight is leaving from. The airport official tells him and wishes him a good trip.

Two spies on an enemy border

One spy gives the other a secret document. Their work is dangerous and they wish each other luck. Then they say good-bye until the next time they meet.

A woman and her elderly father

The old man is going to see a friend in Canada. The daughter wants to make sure her father will be all right. She asks him to call as soon as he arrives.

Two students at the end of the school year

One student is going home after a year in Canada. He/She had a wonderful time with his/her new friends. The other student is sorry to see him/her leave. They both promise to keep in touch.